THE WAR OF INDEPENDENCE

EDWARD PURDON

MERCIER PRESS

CONTENTS

1

RESORT TO ARMS

At Meenbanad, a plateau halfway between Kincasslagh and Dungloe in the Rosses of Donegal, stands a slab monument with the following inscription in Irish and English:

> To commemorate the first action in the War of Independence when the Irish Volunteers rescued two comrades James Ward and James Duffy from British Troops at this place on the 4th day of January 1918.

'This place' was then the last railway halt (known officially as Kincasslagh Road) before the terminus of the Londonderry and Lough Swilly Railway at Burtonport, and the volunteers were removed from the train that was to take them to Derry Jail. The action, carried out by a party of local men that included Fergus Ward and the brothers Dom and John Bonner, antedated by a year and seventeen days the incident that is conventionally regarded as the beginning of the Anglo-Irish War. It was the first of several indications that constitutional methods of achieving the aim of 'old Ireland free' were being thrust aside by the residual Irish Volunteers, soon to call themselves the Irish Republican Army. Unlike the majority of later incidents, it was bloodless – in sharp contrast to the action at Soloheadbeg, County Tipperary, that resulted in the point-blank shooting of two Catholic policemen who were supervising the transport of gelignite to a quarry. This raid, carried out by nine Volunteers, including Dan Breen and Sean Treacy, on 21 January 1919, illustrated the daring and ruthlessness of the Volunteers and marked out members of the Royal Irish Constabulary as the 'enemy' – or the most vulnerable part of it. Like the Meenbanad operation, the Soloheadbeg raid was carried out on local initiative, without sanction from either the Volunteers' central command or Dáil Éireann, the intricately linked parliament which had already formed an alternative system of government.

The RIC had been created as a paramilitary, well-armed force in 1836 (it was called 'royal' from 1867, because of its success in fighting Fenianism) but by the later decades of the nineteenth century it had become essentially a civil constabulary. By 1919 it had many long-serving Catholics, most of them nationalists, and was not equipped to fight a guerrilla war. Its members were conscious, too, that, whatever the outcome of the protracted political process, their days as a force were numbered; uncertainty about the future did not help morale. The other Irish constabulary, the Dublin Metropolitan Police (DMP), had been formed the same year as the RIC, but the members of the DMP prided themselves on being unarmed – and taller and grander than the other force. By the time the truce was – in some cases reluctantly – agreed, on 9 July 1921, the numbers of those killed comprised 428 police (of which ten were DMP officers), 150 military and 750 IRA and civilians.

This last category is necessarily blurred since

it included not only active-service Volunteers and, to use the modern euphemism, 'collateral' casualties but also at least a hundred people that the local IRA commanders designated, often unjustly, as 'spies'. The 'collaterals' included those caught in crossfire, those who had 'failed to halt when challenged' by military or police patrols and, in a few fearsome cases, women and children. The guerrilla war was an often squalid and violent affair, as is inevitably the case with such struggles: participants ruthlessly acted out the logic of their aims; gallantry to defeated enemies was, with rare exceptions, unknown; and reprisals were often out of all proportion to the original events that had triggered them. Life tended to be regarded as cheap: had not millions, including 50,000 Irish nationals, been killed in the previous half-dozen years? Those involved, except for long-serving members of the RIC – mainly young men – found it necessary to stifle normal human feelings; these feelings finally found their outlet in incredulous dismay at the savagery of their opponents and in self-ex-culpatory accounts, both oral and written, composed by participants on both sides long after the time of the actual events.

On the Volunteer side, ancient rage and revenge often caused wanton violence against some 'innocents' who were dimly perceived as being 'on the other side', and the war was used to settle personal grudges as well as to ease an atavistic sense of injustice. The Crown forces, especially the newly created 'Black and Tans' and the even more ruthless 'Auxiliaries', treated the whole population as hostile, and many unarmed civilians were killed in cold blood. Though called a war of independence, the conflict's primary purpose was rendered de facto unachievable by the elections held in May 1921, under the Government of Ireland Act (1920): Ireland was partitioned, and any victory obtained by a continuation of the frightfulness of the war would therefore be incomplete. It was the realisation of this denial of the ultimate ideal that eventually caused the more implacable Volunteers to consider turning from the battle-field to the negotiating table.

The roots of the conflict lay in the British government's attitude to the idea of Irish self-government. Britain had shown a mixture of partiality towards and fear of the unionists from the time of Asquith's Home Rule bill and the signing of the Ulster Covenant in 1912, and had eventually allowed the unionists to control a section of the country that would be politically independent and, with generous subsidies, financially viable. The resulting partition created a state that compromised the northern counties of Antrim, Armagh, Derry, Down, Fermanagh and Tyrone, with a built-in, permanent unionist majority and an equally permanent condition of second-class citizenship for three-quarters of a million nationalists whose homes were in Northern Ireland, as partitioned Ulster was now termed. (Northern Ireland also excluded the considerable Protestant populations of Donegal, Monaghan and Cavan.) The remaining twenty-six counties had been offered such a diluted 'independence' that the words 'home rule' were risible, so that even the conservative Catholic hierarchy refused it. The final rejection of the etiolate proposals of Lloyd George, the British prime minister, was caused by the resounding defeat in the post-war election of the party that had been led by John Redmond until his death on 6 March 1918. He, the heir of O'Connell and Parnell, had done everything he could by constitutional methods to achieve the goal of all Irish leaders since the Act of Union (1801): legislative independence.

The need for the preservation of the Union had exercised the minds of most British (and all Conservative) statesmen since the time of Sir Robert Peel (1788–1850). (It was his name, first associated with the early constabulary, the Peace Preservation Force in 1814, that caused the RIC to be known universally as 'Peelers'.) He believed that, endlessly troublesome as Ireland was (except for the loyal counties of the north-east), this was a small price to pay for the maintenance of the integrity of the growing empire. By the time of the death of the queen in 1901, at the height of Britain's imperial power, the most that even the most liberal politician would contemplate was some kind of weak dominion status for the still-unassimilable Irish. The Great War – and the Easter Rising – changed everything. A significant number of members of Sinn Féin, the group which had replaced Redmond's Irish Parliamentary Party, wanted nothing less than a republic 'virtually established', to use the words of the old IRB oath. The rising had shaken the government and, though conscious that Ireland was the focus of much world attention, especially from the USA, British politicians, even such Liberals as Asquith, made no attempt to conceal their distaste for these nationalist demands.

What increased these politicians' spleen and blunted their normal political acumen was their need to continue a war that they were not winning and which was to cost an enormous number of lives. The principle of 'England's difficulty; Ireland's opportunity' they saw as heinously disloyal, though to the veterans of the Easter Rising and the steadily increasing numbers of the Volunteers it was a simple fact. The movement had recovered quickly from its disarray after the Rising; in some parts of the country, particularly Munster, there was a continuity of arming and public drilling which brought nation-alists into conflict with the police and army. Insensitivity or bloody-mindedness on the part of Lloyd George's government, which was harried by demands from the generals for more soldiers, sharply increased anti-British feeling. The funeral on 25 September 1917 of Thomas Ashe (1885–1917), the hero of the Ashbourne action in Easter Week, who died from pneumonia following forced feeding in Mountjoy Jail, was the occasion of the largest nationalist demonstration seen since Daniel O'Connell's monster meeting at Tara.

The proposal in April 1918 to apply conscription to Ireland, followed by the appointment of the hardline Viscount French as Lord Lieutenant on 11 May 1918, amounted almost to incitement. The logical result of appointing an army general as viceroy is martial law. Lloyd George tried to mitigate the measure by the offer of the immediate implementation of the Home Rule terms that Redmond had agreed to postpone at the outbreak of the war. This offer was manifestly insincere, since it had no unionist support and by now promised too little to have any persuasive force with the rest of the country. French's announcement, made about a week later, that Sinn Féin were in league with the Germans was not even believed by his predecessor, but a hundred leading Volunteers, including Éamon de Valera and Arthur Griffith, were arrested on 17–18 May. The effect of this was to unite nationalist Ireland as never before – and to shift the balance of power in nationalist Ireland to the militants. The anti-conscription campaign was fought by all nationalists groups, with the strong support of the Church and the trade unions, and was eventually successful. The measure (and the promise of Home Rule) was dropped on 20 June, by which time many counties in the west and south were, on French's instructions, under at least partial martial law.

Volunteer tactics required repression for them to succeed; and for the next three years the IRA (as it is convenient to call the military arm of Sinn Féin) and the security forces were in an ironic way collaborators. Ambushes followed by disproportionate reprisals, expressions of national cultural and political will frustrated by draconian oppression, the reputation of both police and army besmirched by gross breaches of discipline – all increased the support for violent tactics. The country which had in general mocked where it did not deplore the 1916 rebels now found itself countenancing much greater violence and tolerating what they would a little earlier have regarded as degraded and criminal. The leaders of the Volunteers, most notably Michael Collins and Cathal Brugha, knew precisely what a guerrilla war entailed and there is a kind of domino inevitability about the sequence of events which led to the struggle for the partial independence that was finally obtained.

It is tempting to think that, because things happened the way they did, no other sequence was possible. In fact there were several possibilities for a more peaceful solution to be reached but a significant number of the new men on the nationalist side were convinced that nothing but a resort to arms would bring the British to their senses. It was an old and a recurring argument, but in this case there existed the will and the means to carry it out – and the necessarily obtuse enemy. Collins had little experience of politics (though he was learning fast) but he was a master of intelligence and the planning of guerrilla tactics. He knew too that, in a country where men were sent to prison for singing seditious songs or giving their names in Irish when accosted by policemen, where there were already easily mobilised local bands of armed zealots and where too long a sacrifice had made a stone of the heart, a war could be started. What he was not sure of was whether it could be finished, or if a majority could stomach what such a war might mean.

The results of the general election in December 1918 were significant not only at home in Ireland – where Sinn Féin secured 73 out of the 105 Irish seats and the old Home Rule party, now led by John Dillon (1851–1927), only six – but also at Westminster, where Lloyd George was returned as head of a coalition dependent on the unionists, led by Bonar Law (1858–1923). The latter had promised total support for Ulster Unionists as early as 1912 and now he left the Welshman with little room to manoeuvre. Lloyd George was inclined to temporise politically while making no effort to stop the spread of martial law and the increasing harassment of ordinary Irish people. Yet, though the extremists would have liked to take the Sinn Féin electoral victory as licence to proceed with a military campaign, many party members had not given up the hope of a constitutional settlement. The party was even regarded among the ordinary people as the best insurance against renewed violence.

Sinn Féin had been founded in 1905 by Arthur Griffith and Bulmer Hobson (1883–1969), a County Down Quaker, as a means of obtaining a kind of independence, by which Ireland should be an equal partner in a dual monarchy under the English crown. The means of obtaining this solution to the perennial Irish question were to be passive resistance and the setting up of alternative institutions to the existing British ones. (The Irish words *sinn féin* mean 'ourselves'.) This approach met with little practical success but its ideas were wrongly assumed by the authorities to be the philosophical basis for the Easter Rising. It was actually the British who reinvigorated the party, by labelling all activists as Sinn Féiners, and contributed to its election success by their betrayal of John Redmond. In fact Sinn Féin members ranged across the whole spectrum of politics and many disapproved of the growing power of the militarists.

Some, particularly de Valera, pinned their hopes on the Paris Peace Conference, which was due to open on 20 January 1919 to consider the rights of 'small nations'. The dominating figure at the conference was to be the American president, Woodrow Wilson (1856–1924), who was assumed, as a Democrat, to be sympathetic to nationalist aspirations. Considering the resolute Presbyterianism of his County Tyrone grandparents and his own instinctive Waspishness, this was an incorrect assumption: Wilson, though happy to be made a freeman of Dublin on 3 January, was clearly reluctant to do anything about a matter that the British delegation insisted was 'internal'. All the members of Sinn Féin, of whatever colour, were determined upon independence and logically set up Dáil Éireann, an independent government that intended to send an independent delegation to Paris (with no success, as it turned out). The president of this government was de Valera, with Collins in charge of finance and Brugha responsible for defence. De Valera was still in jail because of the 'German Plot' and Brugha presided when the Dáil met for the first time on 21 January in the Mansion House in Dawson Street, Dublin. By then, although it was not realised by anyone, the war for independence was two days old, and it had not been declared by Sinn Féin.

2

TARGETS

Sean Treacy, the leader of the Soloheadbeg ambush, had initiated the war for independence because, as he put it, 'It was high time we did a bit of pushing.' Dan Breen gave a more sober version of events: 'The Volunteers were in great danger of becoming merely a political adjunct to the Sinn Féin organization.' The nine participants were local: both Breen and Treacy lived close to the quarry to which the 168 pounds of gelignite and thirty-eight detonators were being conveyed by horse and cart from the military barracks in Tipperary. Two RIC constables, fifty-seven-year-old James McDonnell, a married man from County Mayo, and thirty-six-year-old Patrick O'Donnell, a bachelor from County Cork, were sent along as guards with the driver, Patrick Godfrey. They were met at the entrance to the quarry by the county council employee, Patrick Flynn, who was to take delivery. The constables fell dead in a hail of rifle and revolver shots, and, in the confusion of collecting the police rifles and gelignite, Breen's mask slipped, thus enabling the authorities to use his photograph on reward posters offering £1,000 for information leading to his capture.

Though it was the first – and an entirely unauthorised – action in the struggle, this episode shared one feature with other similar attacks: local intelligence was of good quality. The South Tipperary Brigade were told that a consignment of explosives would 'soon be on its way to the quarry' and so the ambush party was in position on each day from dawn on 16 January, leaving the scene around 2 pm in the afternoon. Local and national reaction was one of almost universal condemnation. The constables had been popular members of a small-town community; a relief fund for McDonnell's family (he left a wife and five children) was set up immediately. The local clergy and Dr Harty, the Archbishop of Cashel, declared the action morally wrong. It was also condemned by Sinn Féin and leading members of the IRB, though whether the disapproval by these last two was of the action or its freelance nature is unclear. Certainly *An tÓglach*, the IRB journal edited by Piaras Beaslaí, announced on 31 January that Volunteers were entitled morally and politically to inflict death on the enemies of the State: 'soldiers and policemen of the British Government'.

The next RIC casualty was Constable Martin O'Brien, who was shot on 6 April during an attempt by a Limerick City company of the IRA to rescue Robert Byrne, a republican hunger striker, from St Camillus' Hospital. Like south Tipperary after Soloheadbeg and Westport after the shooting of a magistrate on 31 March, the area was proclaimed a military area. Though all these deaths were greeted with genuine revulsion, the swamping of the areas with military and police checkpoints, the humiliating body searches, the requirement of permits for journeys or even the driving of stock to market and the general interference with ordinary life soon blunted the regret. It seemed that the British government had learned nothing, not even the wisdom of allowing the local and generally tactful RIC to continue to maintain order.

The Soloheadbeg team went into action again on 13 May, rescuing Sean Hogan from the Thurles–Cork train at Knocklong station, just over the county boundary in Limerick. As a result of the action, Sergeant Peter Wallace and Constable Michael Enright died from gunshot wounds and Breen himself was so severely wounded that he was not expected to survive. Again there was strong condemnation of the shootings, with Dr Harty denouncing the action and urging Irishmen 'not to stain the fair name of their native land with deeds of blood'. In all, fifteen policemen were killed in 1919, including a district inspector, Michael Hunt, after the Thurles Races on 23 June. More significantly, two of those who lost their lives were DMP detectives: DS Patrick Smyth (killed on 30 July) and DC Daniel Hoey (12 September). These were part of the city police force's G-Division, the plain-clothes members of which were called G-men (long before the members of J. Edgar Hoover's FBI were known by the same name). They were the first victims of Collins's deadly band of counter-intelligence operatives, known as 'the Squad'.

Collins was enough of a student of Irish history to realise that, in all previous Irish insurrections – that of the United Irishmen in 1798, Robert Emmet's in 1803, William Smith O'Brien's in 1848 and the Fenian outbreak in 1867 – government intelligence agents had discovered the details of plans and personnel well in advance of the attack. He was determined to reverse this situation by building up his own network of spies and counter-intelligence operatives. The Squad was essentially a band of expert gunmen officially formed in September 1919, though a notional Squad existed before that. Dick McKee, one of Collins's chief aides, who helped train them, had warned prospective members that those with scruples about taking life should not join. DS Smyth was a very effective detective, known as 'Dog' Smyth because of his sleuthing ability. Like many G-men, he had been warned by some of Collins's men that he should be less assiduous in his work but he persisted and was shot by five gunmen after alighting from a tram at Drumcondra Bridge. He returned fire and managed to reach his home before collapsing. DC Hoey had been an intended target of Collins ever since he had picked out Sean MacDermott (1884–1916), one of the leaders of the 1916 Rising, from the crowd of Volunteers who were to be shipped to the relative safety of an English prison. Mac-Dermott was executed in Kilmainham on 12 May 1916 and the name of Hoey was filed away in Collins's prodigious memory for future action. Hoey was shot as he entered the police station in Brunswick Street on the day that the government proscribed Dáil Éireann.

One of Collins's most effective Castle spies was Ned Broy. He had joined the DMP in 1911 and served as a sergeant-clerk in G-division. His usual technique was to slip an extra carbon and flimsy into his typewriter for every document he dealt with and pass the copy to Collins later that evening. It was from Broy that Collins got the list of those whom the government intended to arrest because of the 'German Plot'. As a result, Collins was able to warn de Valera and the rest of the Volunteer Executive at their meeting on 17 May 1918 that they were likely to be arrested. For reasons that can be guessed, de Valera went home; a few days later he found himself a prisoner in Lincoln Jail. His rescue from prison on 3 February 1919 became part of the Collins legend, with all the ripping-yarns paraphernalia of keys made from wax impressions which broke in the lock and the prisoner walking arm in arm with one of his rescuers past groups of courting Tommies and their sweethearts.

De Valera was the obvious leader of the Irish forces: he was a veteran of Easter Week, probably the most successful military commander on the Irish side and a politician with a remarkably supple, not to say Machiavellian, mind. He was famous for recommending Richard Mulcahy, the Volunteer Chief of Staff, to read *Il Principe*, and ever since the Rising he had shown a distrust of violence. He was also immovable once he had made a decision. Instead of staying at home to organise the 'war' that was brewing, he insisted on going to America. The decision caused the rest of the Executive some dismay, especially those, like Griffith (released in the general amnesty in March), who wished to hold the militant wing of Sinn Féin in check. In fact, de Valera leaving left Collins free to conduct the war as he saw fit. He knew the propaganda and morale-boosting value of the 'spectacular' to complement the series of raids and ambushes being carried on by individual IRA brigades and it seemed to him that the most spectacular action might be the successful assassination of the Viceroy. John French had gone to his home in Roscommon and was on his way back to Dublin on 19 December. An ambush was laid near the viceregal lodge in Phoenix Park but the only casualty was a Volunteer named Savage who was caught in crossfire. When, on 21 December, the *Irish Independent* described Savage as 'a would-be assassin', the paper's offices and presses were destroyed by a party of Volunteers.

Action was not confined to the IRA: at least some attempt was made at setting up Griffith's counter-state. As well as being virtual commander of operations, Collins was Minister of Finance in the Dáil, and he raised £380,000 in redeemable bonds repayable by the future independent Ireland. (He also discovered during the flotation that most ordinary people are slow to part with money for any cause.) Sinn Féin soon controlled so many councils as to give them control of local government. Rates were no longer paid and arbitration courts, whose decisions were binding, were preferred to the state ones. There was even an attempt made to set up a Sinn Féin police force. This 'dry-run' at self-government increased confidence sufficiently that post-Treaty Ireland was governed with an unexpected efficiency.

3

BLACK AND TANS – AND AUXIES

The year 1920 began with the ominous arrival in Ireland of the new RIC recruits, intended to supplement the native Irish force, which was then reeling from IRA attacks and social ostracism. The total numbers who left the force in 1919 for all causes was 495, of which only 99 had resigned. The equivalent figures for 1920 were 3,229, with almost exactly half that number of resignations and 178 killed in action. The order for supplementary recruitment was issued on 2 January and by 21 November 1921 the force's numbers had reached 9,500. The personnel were ex-soldiers and ex-sailors who, unemployed and finding life dull after the excitement of the war, were happy to become mercenaries for ten shillings a day and all-found. The urgency was such that complete uniforms could not be found for the first draft. They wore dark green police hats and belts over khaki uniforms and made no attempt to hide their military nature. They first appeared on patrol in Upper Church, County Tipperary, where there was a famous local pack of hounds called the 'Black and Tans'; the name was applied to the new recruits and it stuck. In spite of the equally foul reputation of the Auxiliary Cadets, who were first recruited in July 1920, the struggle of 1920–21 became known as the 'Tan war'.

In spite of contemporary belief, the vetting process at recruitment was nearly as strict as for ordinary RIC officers. There may have been some few with a criminal record but most were young men who were only too happy to engage in the reprisals that were at first condoned and eventually openly approved by the increasingly desperate authorities. The 'sweepings of English jails' – the usual nationalist jibe – was an inaccurate description but many of the exploits of the new recruits were criminal if viewed in absolute terms. They were badly trained and, apart from the perhaps one-quarter of them who were native Irish recruits, had no experience or knowledge of the country in which they found themselves. Even the Irish recruits, who were mainly of Ulster origin, would have found Munster and west Connacht, the main places of deployment outside of Dublin, somewhat alien. The force's pied appearance did not last; by the end of 1920 uniforms were again uniform and it was impossible to tell the strangers from the regular RIC, except by accent and, some would say, by behaviour.

In fact the first piece of serious breach of police discipline took place before the 'Tans' were mobilised. On 22 January twenty-nine-year-old Constable Michael Finnegan was walking home to the Mall in Thurles when he was shot by three men. The local police immediately went on the rampage, shooting out the windows of twelve prominent Sinn Féiners and throwing grenades through the office window of the *Tipperary Star*. This action was on a small scale compared with later excesses. The day before the Thurles incident, the Squad had struck at their most senior target: William Redmond, the Assistant Commissioner of the DMP, who had been put in charge of the demoralised G Division, was shot in the back as he walked from the Castle to his hotel in Harcourt Street.

On the night of 19–20 March, after the shooting of Constable Joseph Murtagh in Pope's Quay, Cork, a band of armed men with blackened faces and in civilian clothes burst into the home of Tomás MacCurtain, the Sinn Féin lord mayor of the city. They rushed straight upstairs and shot him in his bed. The inquest returned a verdict of wilful murder against 'David Lloyd George, Prime Minister of England, Lord French, Lord Lieutenant of Ireland, Ian Mac Pherson, Late Chief Secretary of Ireland, Acting Inspector General Smith of the RIC, Divisional Inspector Clayton of the RIC, DI Swanzy and some unknown members of the RIC'. The authorities tried to say that the perpetrators had been members of the IRB, who were impatient at MacCurtain's lack of support for the campaign, but no one believed the story. Swanzy was placed on Collins's mental list of enemies to be eliminated; he was shot in Lisburn, County Antrim, on 22 August. The aftermath was serious sectarian rioting in Lisburn and Belfast.

Most Catholic houses in Lisburn were destroyed and there were twenty-four civilian deaths. These riots, together with the even more savage ones in Derry earlier in the summer, led to the recruitment of men for the Ulster Special Constabularies; the most notorious of these, the 'B' Specials, manned by part-time loyalists, were to continue as a notably partial force until their final disbandment in 1970.

The shock of MacCurtain's death and the evidence of RIC involvement in the crime was mitigated somewhat by the killing by the Squad of Alan Bell on 26 March. Bell was an elderly magistrate who was part of French's counter-espionage team. He was known to have been successful in finding evidence of Sinn Féin bank accounts. He used to travel each day by tram from his home in Monkstown without a guard. That morning four members of the Squad took him off the tram at Ballsbridge and shot him. Another high-profile incident had a less bloody conclusion. A General Lucas was captured by an IRA platoon led by Liam Lynch (1893–1923) while fishing on the Blackwater, near Fermoy, County Cork, on 26 July. He was moved around for a month until his guard, Michael Brennan, tired of supplying him with a daily bottle of whiskey paid for out of Brennan's own pocket, allowed him to escape. Relations between the general and his captors were genial; he played tennis, made hay and wrote and received daily letters from his wife. They took him salmon poaching one night and he was relieved to see that the IRA boatman was the river bailiff. On the darker side, the general's troops went on the rampage in Fermoy and other towns (a rare example of military response) in reprisal for the kidnapping, although, unlike in Tan and Auxiliary raids, no one was killed.

The Auxies – the Auxiliary Division of the RIC – were the brainchild of Winston Churchill, Minister of War and the Air in Lloyd George's coalition. They were ex-British Army officers and, with permission to wear either army uniform (without insignia) or police uniform, they were literally 'Black and Tan'; their distinguishing feature was the wearing of Glengarry bonnets. Later they had distinctive blue uniforms with black chest bandoliers and leather belts holding bayonets and open holsters with .45 revolvers.

Most had been high-ranking officers and many had been decorated for valour, including two holders of the VC and many DSOs, MCs and holders of the Croix de Guerre. Their reputation in Ireland, however, was of drunkenness, brutality and lack of discipline, to the extent that their commander, General Frank Crozier, resigned on 19 February 1921, a mere six and a half months after taking command. They were meant as quick-response, motorised units of a hundred men whose targets were the newly organised IRA flying squads, which operated mainly in Munster.

The most notorious examples of reprisals were the 'sackings' of various Irish towns. Typical was the Auxiliary action in Balbriggan, County Dublin, on 20 September 1920. Head Constable Peter Burke and his brother Michael, a sergeant, were shot with dum-dum bullets in a public house. Peter died on the spot but Michael later recovered from his wounds. Peter had been involved in training the Auxiliary Division in the Phoenix Park depot. A party of Auxiliaries arrived from Gormanston and, on seeing, it is said, their old instructor lying dead, wreaked destruction on property with grenades, setting many houses on fire and savagely killing two civilians with bayonets. The scene was marked by lines of refugees fleeing from their ravaged town. From this time the beleaguered inhabitants of towns and villages where reprisals were expected took to leaving their homes at sundown and spending the night in what safety they could find in hedges and barns. Similar scenes followed the killing of a sergeant and five constables at Rineen, between Milltown Malbay and Lahinch, County Clare, the next day. Houses were burnt in the nearby towns and four people were killed, including one who tried to help a neighbour put out the fire in his house. On 28 September Liam Lynch and Ernie O'Malley (1898–1957) captured the RIC barracks in Mallow, County Cork. During the raid an army sergeant was killed, and later that evening the army ravaged the town. Two days later it was the turn of Trim, County Meath, when the town was wrecked and the shops looted by Tans after the RIC barracks was set on fire by the IRA.

4

BLOODY SUNDAY

The autumn of 1920 and the spring of 1921 were to prove the bloodiest periods of the war. They were characterised by attacks on barracks, now fortified by barbed wire and sandbags, as well as ambushes, reprisals and counter-reprisals, intimidation and physical violence inflicted by both sides on civilians, and a swift descent into terror for the parts of the country where there was IRA activity. The cities of Cork, Limerick and Dublin and the counties of Cork, Tipperary, Kerry, Limerick, Clare, Roscommon and Donegal bore the brunt of the fighting. Yet even there, large areas were unaffected, except by dread and rumour, and the inconvenience of military restrictions. Between January 1919 and the Truce in July 1921 there were 136 recorded IRA operations in Cork but the north of the county was relatively quiet; Tipperary had fifty-eight, Kerry forty-four, Limerick thirty-three, Clare twenty-five and Donegal eleven. Thirty-nine policemen were killed in Ulster, eight in Belfast and four in Derry, with the remainder mainly in the border regions of Armagh, Cavan, Monaghan and Donegal. One was a head constable and seven were 'specials' who had been commissioned after November 1920. IRA activity was generally light in the north until 1922 but attacks on police continued there after the Truce and the setting up of the Northern Ireland state on 1 June. Between then and the time of the death of the last recorded casualty, Special Constable Samuel Hayes, who was shot in the Newtownards Road, Belfast on 5 August, seven officers were killed.

Though official sanction for reprisals was not given until January 1922, there was little attempt at investigating those responsible for the indiscriminate killing of civilians. After Balbriggan, Sir Hamar Greenwood, the chief secretary, who had been appointed on 4 April 1920 and whose public utterances became so specious that 'telling a Hamar' became a euphemism for lying, told the House of Commons that it was 'impossible' to find out who was responsible for the burning, looting and killing. The implicit policy had been baldly stated by Lt Col Brice Smyth, the RIC divisional commander for Munster, at Listowel on 9 June. In an address to a group of RIC officers he urged them to be ruthless: 'The more you shoot the better I will like you, and no policeman will get into trouble for shooting a man.' He also hinted at the vicious treatment that was being meted out to IRA prisoners and, since their purpose was to wipe out Sinn Féin, 'any man who is not prepared to do this is a hindrance, and had better leave the job at once.' One courageous constable did just that: Jeremiah Mee walked up to the table and threw his revolver and cap upon it, saying that Smyth's speech was incitement to murder. Smyth ordered his arrest but nobody moved. The incident became known as the 'Listowel Mutiny' and the highly decorated one-armed veteran was added to Collins's list. Mee and several colleagues resigned on 6 July and Smyth was killed in the smoking room of the Cork Country Club eleven days later by members of the Cork No. 1 Brigade. Mee was recruited by Collins as a propagandist to tour the United States with tales of the government policy of atrocity – ironically, as it now seems, since Collins's policy was not notably different from the government's.

Major George Smyth, who was then serving in Egypt, on hearing of the death of his brother applied for a transfer to Irish intelligence, bringing with him, it is said, eleven comrades for the sole intention of avenging the killing, which he blamed, incorrectly, on Dan Breen. Breen and Treacy had been active in Dublin since the failed attempt on French's life in which they had taken part; they were doughty fighters and Collins wanted to keep them under his direct control. The arrival of Smyth in Dublin coincided with the effective reorganisation of government intelligence by Brig Gen Sir Ormonde Winter, known to the Squad as the 'Holy Terror'. His agents had located Breen and Treacy at a house in Whitehall. In the raid which took place on 10 October, Smyth and another officer were killed, and the householder, Professor John Carolan of St Patrick's Training

College, put against the wall and shot in the head, but the two Volunteers, in spite of serious wounds, escaped. The funeral of Smyth, fixed for 14 October, was expected to be a solemn affair, with General Neville Macready (British Commander-in-Chief since April) and General Henry Tudor (Commander of the RIC) in attendance. It was too good an opportunity for Collins to miss. The Squad, with Treacy among them, attended but, probably on Winter's advice, the generals stayed away. Treacy was recognised in the doorway of the Republican Outfitters, run by Dublin IRA officer Peadar Clancy, and was shot during a raid. Major Smyth's body was taken to Banbridge, County Down, to be buried in the family plot beside his brother.

Two other 'names' of Volunteer mythology were to die that autumn: Terence MacSwiney, who had succeeded MacCurtain as lord mayor of Cork, died on 25 October after seventy-four days on hunger strike; and Kevin Barry, an eighteen-year-old medical student, was hanged for being in possession of a gun at the scene of the killing of an even younger soldier on 20 September. Barry bequeathed one of the long-surviving ballads of the period ('Another martyr for old Ireland; another murder for the Crown') and MacSwiney set a pattern for future republicans.

Both deaths increased the surge of world opinion against Britain. The *Manchester Guardian* and the *Daily News* (whose literary editor, Robert Lynd, had been a member of the original Sinn Féin and a friend of Roger Casement) attacked the government constantly, effectively neutralising the rabid anti-Irish propaganda of the *Morning Post* and the *Spectator*. The most telling propaganda sheet was the *Irish Bulletin,* put out by Desmond Fitzgerald (1889–1947), Frank Gallagher and Erskine Childers. The *Bulletin* had even more impact abroad than at home. Its experienced journalists – Childers had written the best-selling *The Riddle of the Sands* (1903), which anticipated Germany's entry into the Great War – were able to depict Volunteer successes as heroic and condemn government actions as squalidly savage. As a result of such publicity, de Valera was able to win a great deal of sympathy in America for the Irish cause – as well as securing $5 million for use in Ireland.

Lloyd George was no longer able to close his eyes and wish the Irish problem would go away.

The worst month of 1920 proved to be November; it was in fact probably the worst month in the whole struggle. In the early morning of 21 November the Squad killed eleven members of the British secret service in their homes and hotels. Two Auxiliaries, Frank Garniss and Cecil Morris, who happened to be on the scene of one of the killings in Lower Mount Street, were themselves killed; they were the first Auxiliary fatalities. Two of Collins's closest aides, Dick McKee and Peadar Clancy, who had been arrested the previous evening, were 'shot while trying to escape'. So 'Bloody Sunday' began. It was the day of a football final between Dublin and Tipperary, and Croke Park was crowded that afternoon. The grounds were surrounded by Crown forces in the likely anticipation of their finding Volunteers among the crowd. Against instructions, a party of Auxiliaries drove into the ground while the match was in progress. Predictably, they claimed they had been fired on from the crowd; what is certain is that they turned their guns on the teams and shot into the stands. Twelve people died – some from bullets, others trampled to death as the hysterical crowd tried to find cover. The fatalities included a woman, a child and one of the Tipperary forwards.

These events, which in a sense cancelled each other out in terms of their horror, received worldwide publicity, thus edging Lloyd George, with infinite slowness, towards tentative moves to a truce. These moves stopped again when, one week later, Tom Barry's west Cork flying column ambushed an Auxiliary patrol at Kilmichael. The cadets were under the command of DI F. W. Crake and travelled in two Crossley tenders on their usual triangular sweep: Macroom, Dunmanway, Bandon and back to Macroom. Barry had begun training his men on Bloody Sunday and chose a stretch of bogland near Kilmichael, eight miles from Macroom. Eighteen Auxiliaries were killed – some by Mills bombs and others, it was insisted by the government information offices, after they had surrendered. There were accusations, too, of mutilations of the bodies of the dead using axes and of the stealing of personal possessions.

Barry himself said that all the dead had been killed in the fighting and that the Auxiliaries had used a favourite trick of the false surrender, which had resulted in the deaths of two Volunteers.

A reprisal, perhaps the most notorious of all, came two weeks later, on Saturday 11 December, when, after an ambush at Dillon's Cross in Cork in which an Auxiliary was killed and ten of his companions wounded, the centre of the city was set on fire by a combined force of drunken Tans and cadets. They prevented the fire service from reaching the sites of many of the blazes and looted what they could from the burning stores. Afterwards Auxiliaries swaggered around Dublin with burnt corks on their Glengarries. Greenwood had to tell another 'Hamar' in the House, claiming, with enviable effrontery, that the city had been torched by its own citizens. The report of the military enquiry undertaken by General Strickland, the OC for the Cork district, was never published because its effect 'would be disastrous to the government's whole policy in Ireland'. Three million pounds was paid later in compensation.

Lloyd George was out to please his audience when he claimed at the yearly Guildhall banquet in the City of London on 9 November: 'We have murder by the throat.' He used the occasion to exonerate those Crown forces who were guilty of excesses in Ireland and gave a hint that they should be given a freer rein in the future. His suggestion of an official sanction for reprisals and the treating of the Volunteers as criminals was also to please his Minister of Defence, Winston Churchill, who, though a Liberal since 1906, was already giving clear indications of his intention to rejoin the Tory party of his 'Orange card'-playing father, Lord Randolph (1849–95). It was Churchill who insisted that Kevin Barry be hanged as a murderer and who prompted J. H. Thomas, who was afterwards to be Dominions Minister in Ramsay MacDonald's first Labour government, to condemn the execution in the House.

Lloyd George knew that, if the killings by the IRA were murders, then so too were those carried out by his forces in Ireland. There was a deal of semantic shuffling as to what was the exact nature of the crimes of the IRA. They insisted – and truly believed – that they were fighting a glorious war finally to free Ireland from English rule and that they were right to declare Ireland as a 'virtually established' republic. Yet it would have been 'dignifying the action of murderers' for the government to elevate the IRA's guerrilla activity to the level of legitimate conflict – despite the fact that such a recognition would have given the army generals a freer hand in dealing with insurgents. As it was, the generals continually felt themselves shackled by political restraints; even the go-ahead for 'official' reprisals contained implicit conditions.

The horrors of the year were not over yet: Canon Magner, PP of Dunmanway and a young parishioner of his, Timothy Crowley, were shot dead by an Auxiliary officer on 15 December because the priest had not tolled his church bells on Armistice Day. This happened exactly a month after the body of Fr Michael Griffin, a priest from Barna, County Galway, with known Volunteer sympathies, had been found riddled with bullets near his home the day after his arrest by Crown forces. Nineteen twenty headed towards its murky close with two incidents that were entirely characteristic of its terror. On 27 December the RIC carried out a raid on a Big House, left vacant by its owners, at Bruff, County Limerick, where a dance was being held to raise funds for the East Limerick Third Battalion of the IRA. Five IRA men were shot and seventeen injured, and two Tans were killed in the assault. Then, on 29 December, three Tans on patrol in Midleton, County Cork, were shot; they eventually died of their injuries. The town was to be the scene of the first 'official reprisal' by soldiers on 1 January 1921, when seven houses were destroyed. Another year of apparently endless violence had begun.

5

TRUCE

The last six months of the war were its bloodiest and most squalid: the number of police casualties from January to July was 235 – 57 more than for the whole of 1920; 707 civilians were killed and 756 wounded. Of the civilians killed, more than a hundred were shot by the IRA as spies – a term that often meant refusal to cooperate with the local brigade, as when a labourer was shot for filling in a trench dug by local Volunteers. An even greater number were deliberately shot by Crown forces. Young men were particularly at risk from Tans and Auxiliaries, whose lack of discipline and lawlessness eventually caused the latter's commander, Brig Gen Frank Crozier, to resign on 19 February after his dismissals had been overruled by General Tudor, the head of police. His rejection of them as 'a drunken and insubordinate body of men' was no surprise to the people of Ireland and was officially ignored by the government. Yet it was another blow against Lloyd George's conduct of Irish affairs and a further stimulus to the moves to seek some cessation of the violence.

Female fatalities, till then the result of being caught in crossfire, now happened as part of raids. On 14 May 1921 DI Harry Biggs and the daughter of Sir Charles Barrington were killed on the way home from a fishing expedition at Newport, County Tipperary; two other women and an army officer escaped unharmed. The next day DI Blake and his wife were killed (she was shot five times) when their car was ambushed coming home from a tennis match at Gort, County Galway. (The number of police fatalities for that May – fifty-six – was the greatest for any month of the conflict.) The incident that caused the greatest revulsion was the kidnapping and shooting of an elderly woman, Mrs Lindsay, who had reported to the authorities that an ambush was being prepared near her home at Coachford, County Cork. On foot of the information she passed on, seven IRA men were apprehended and executed in Cork on 5 February; that same evening six unarmed soldiers were killed in Cork city.

IRA ambushes (the numbers of the ambush parties often heavily outnumbering their targets) and individual assassinations continued as did Tan and Auxiliary raids. On 7 March the Sinn Féin mayor of Limerick, George Clancy, former mayor Michael O'Callaghan and Joseph O'Donoghue were shot dead in their homes, almost a year after Tomás MacCurtain had been dispatched in a similar fashion. There was a half-hearted attempt made to discipline the Tans and Auxiliaries: the 'official' reprisal in Midleton, County Cork, on 1 January was the last of its kind but more and more of the country was placed under martial law.

The presence of de Valera, who had returned from America on 23 December 1920, was beginning to have an effect. He was utterly intractable once he had made a decision and, though it seemed odd that he found it necessary to spend nineteen months away from the racked country, no one, least of all Collins, cared either to try to prevent his going to America or to comment upon the length of his stay there. As ever, de Valera showed a less than noble capacity for making sure he would not be held responsible for hard decisions. He was deeply concerned about the effect that the campaign was having upon the country and rather surprised at the position that Collins had secured for himself. De Valera had little taste for guerrilla fighting; the lack of military uniform, though a considerable advantage for the IRA, meant that there could be no appeal to the Geneva Convention about such things as prisoners' rights. Greenwood had made it clear that the 5,000 internees in camps like Ballykinlar, near Dundrum in County Down, would receive prisoner-of-war treatment without being given POW status.

De Valera's time in America had toughened him politically; he found he was no match for the tough Irish-American career politicians who, among other things, wished to wreck the League of Nations – Woodrow Wilson's great hope for lasting peace. Wilson, heavily incapacitated in his last months of office by a stroke, was of no help when it came to securing recognition of

Ireland's right to independence, and when, in November 1919, the Republican W. G. Harding (1865–1923) was elected president on an isolationist ticket without a single mention of Ireland during his campaign, it was clear that Ireland could expect no official support from America. As Harding said, when asked to support Irish independence, 'I would not care to undertake to say to Great Britain what she must do, any more than I would permit her to tell us what we must do with the Philippines.'

De Valera, with his innate distrust of lawlessness, wanted to set the IRA's activities on a moral basis, regardless of the fact that the lack of such a foundation for their actions did not worry Collins or Brugha (who were now drifting apart), let alone the various brigades. As *príomhaire* of Dáil Éireann, de Valera was in a position to insist that a formal state of war be declared against Britain and on 11 March the proclamation was made. He urged a cutting-back in IRA activity, as if that were either practicable or popular: 'What we want is one good battle with about 500 men on each side.' Such a 'good battle' actually took place, at his urging, on 25

May, when the Customs House, where many local-government records were stored, was occupied and burned by the IRA. Troops and Auxiliaries surrounded the building before the raiding party could escape. Five Volunteers were killed and eighty taken prisoner – and one of Dublin's architectural glories burned for five days. From Collins's point of view the action was a military disaster and did nothing to improve relations between him and de Valera, who were now quite obviously at odds. Yet coming when it did at a time when Lloyd George's government could no longer bear the shadows on its reputation abroad, especially in America, it proved to be a political triumph.

Lloyd George's position within the coalition had not improved, even though one of the hawks had turned into a dove. Churchill, whose political antennae were even more sensitive than de Valera's, came out strongly in favour of a truce. The prime minister's own Liberal Party was now in a minority and dependent on the grace and favour of Arthur Balfour (1848–1930), leader of the Conservatives, and the unionist Bonar Law. Lloyd George also had to face down his often baying, red-faced generals, who always said they could finish the thing if he removed the political constraints under which they operated. Truce negotiations were conducted with all the formality and indecision of a seventeenth-century court minuet. Even as Lloyd George was prating about having 'murder by the throat' he was testing the possibilities of compromise, and many worthy people worked tirelessly to effect a solution. One was the Archbishop of Perth, P. J. Clune, whose nephew, a civilian Gaelic Leaguer, had been arrested in the same hotel as McKee and Clancy, and like them had been 'shot while trying to escape'. Clune's efforts failed when Lloyd George refused to deal with the rebels before they gave up their arms – a song that is being heard again!

Negotiations were continued mainly by 'Andy' Cope, who was the joint Irish under-secretary and one of the tireless heroes of the process. The arrest on 22 June of de Valera, who was now president of the second Dáil – which had 124 Sinn Féin members, all elected unopposed – was an embarrassment that Cope had to deal with. De Valera was released the next day. Another nationalist objection to the process was the refusal to allow Collins to be a party to peace talks. Under the Government of Ireland Act, if Southern Ireland would not accept an agreed self-government, it would revert to the position of a crown colony, which would have meant the entire twenty-six counties being under martial law; it was reckoned that this would require 100,000 troops to maintain. With no let-up in IRA activity and deafening criticism even from the British newspapers, the pressure to treat eventually became overwhelming. George V's speech at the opening of the Belfast parliament in the City Hall on 22 June, written for him by Lloyd George, with a significant contribution by Jan Smuts, finally persuaded the British people that the time had come for peace. The king urged 'all Irishmen to pause, to stretch out the hand of forbearance and conciliation, to forgive and forget and to join in making for the land which they love a new era of peace, contentment and goodwill.'

The IRA, especially those members in the south and west, who were by now veteran warriors, were not likely to be impressed by such sentiments, expressed by such a person in such a place on the occasion of the formal partitioning of the country. They were, however, in need of respite: Collins reckoned that resistance could not have continued for more than three weeks. Lloyd George had removed all his previous conditions about personnel and the laying down of arms and, although de Valera was at his most byzantine in terms of the conditions he imposed, a truce concluded in the Mansion House between Macready and his aide Col Brind and Éamonn Duggan and Robert Barton came into effect on 11 July. The conditions included a cessation of attacks on Crown forces and civilians, the avoidance of provocative displays of force and no reinforcements of men or arms by either side; the provisions were to apply to the area under martial law as well as the rest of the country.

The truce was fragile but it held. Collins and the other leaders understood the risk the IRA took 'like rabbits coming out of their holes' and many were confused. The last killing was of four unarmed soldiers at 9 pm the night before the truce was signed; the last policemen, Constable Alexander Clarke, had been shot that afternoon in Skibbereen. It took some time for the realisation that the country was again at peace to sink in. One slightly cynical, if not unexpected, result of the end of hostilities was the increase in numbers joining the IRA – the 'Trucileers', as the famous and ubiquitous anonymous Irish wit was to call them. Those who had fought in constant danger of their lives on both sides were glad of at least a temporary lull; ominous cracks were already beginning to appear in the smooth façade of IRA unity. No revolution can be entirely bloodless, and worse was to come.

Yet throughout the twenty-six counties there was a light-headed sense that maybe now things would get better. The war had generated plenty of new heroes – Tom Barry, Liam Deasy, Sean Treacy, Dan Breen, Ernie O'Malley, Oscar Traynor (1886–1963), Liam Lynch, Sean Mac-Eoin (1893–1973), and many others whose story was not yet complete. Not all the Volunteers were heroes and not all their adversaries were villains. Some names live in local infamy; some were – and still are – granted a grudging respect. One egregious exception to this was Major Arthur Percival of the Essex regiment, who liked to ride about south Cork in an open car with a loaded gun in his hands, looking for targets. He was undoubtedly responsible for the torture of prisoners and was lucky to escape with his life. He did live to face the humiliation, as Lt General Percival, of surrendering his army to the much smaller Japanese force in Singapore on 15 February 1942 after 'the greatest military defeat in the history of the British Empire'.

When the terms of the truce were published, there followed a week of rioting in Belfast. Members of the new Special Constabulary, mostly recruited from the UVF, joined forces with Protestant mobs over the Twelfth holiday. Sixteen Catholics and seven Protestants were killed and over 200 Catholic homes were destroyed. There was nothing new in anti-Catholic pogroms but the appalled minority nationalist population was beginning to understand what the Government of Ireland Act was to mean to them. The Volunteers and their late adversaries had other things on their minds but the news from the North should have concentrated the minds of the peacemakers. It is, even at this distance, hard to understand why they had so little understanding of the Ulster unionists and why they allowed the promise of a boundary commission to blind their eyes to the real flaw in the treaty terms. The Volunteers were entitled to their moment of triumph; they were yet to learn the truth of the final words of David Neligan, one of Collins's Castle moles, in his book *The Spy in the Castle:* 'Revolution devours her own children.'

BIOGRAPHICAL INDEX

Kevin Barry (1902–20) was born in Dublin and joined the Irish Volunteers in 1917 while still at Belvedere. On 20 September 1920, while a medical student at UCD, he took part in an ambush in which an even younger soldier was killed. Found hiding under a cart in possession of a revolver, Barry was sentenced to be hanged. His execution, on I November, prompted widespread criticism.

Tom Barry (1897–1980) was born in Rosscarbery, County Cork, the son of a policeman who had bought a pub on his retirement. He joined the army in 1915 and served at Ypres and later in Mesopotamia. Two years after the war he enrolled in a business college in Cork but was approached by Volunteers as a man of known military experience. Soon he had trained his own highly disciplined West Cork flying column – a concept in guerrilla warfare he largely developed himself. In November 1920 he led the Kilmichael ambush, in which the Auxiliaries suffered their most serious defeat, and on March 1921 at Crossbarry successfully engaged a superior force from the Essex regiment. He took the anti-Treaty side in the Civil War and continued as a member of the IRA until 1938, when he resigned because he disagreed with the organisation's bombing campaign in Britain. He subsequently published *Guerrilla Days in Ireland* (1949), an inevitably partisan account of his activities as a flying-column leader.

Robert Barton (1881–1975), a cousin of Erskine Childers*, was born in County Wicklow and educated at Rugby and Oxford. He resigned from the British Army in 1916 and joined the IRA. Minister for Agriculture in the first Dáil, he worked out the terms of the truce which ended the War of Independence in 1921. He was one of the signatories of the Treaty, recommending it as 'the lesser of two outrages', but remained a supporter of de Valera*. He was chairman of the Agricultural Credit Corporation (1934–54) and later of Bord na Móna.

Piaras Béaslaí (1881–1965) was born in Liverpool and moved to Dublin in 1904. He considered the Gaelic League an important part of the independence movement and helped change its apolitical stance. He was a commander in the Easter Rising and was editor of *An tÓglach* and IRA director of publicity from February 1921. He supported the Treaty and served as commandant-general in the Free State army. Resigning in 1924, he became a writer and Gaelic scholar, and Michael Collins's* first biographer.

Dan Breen (1894–1969) was a farmer's son, born in Soloheadbeg, County Tipperary, the scene of the attack on a party of RIC men – in which he and Sean Treacy* were involved – on 21 January 1919 that is taken as being the first action in the War of Independence. They were also active in Dublin, making an attempt on the life of the Lord Lieutenant, among other things. He continued guerrilla activity in Tipperary during the Civil War until he was captured on 17 April 1923. He was the first opponent of the Treaty to sit in the Dáil, taking his seat in

January 1927. He served as Fianna Fáil TD for Tipperary South from 1932 to 1965. His autobiography, *My Fight for Irish Freedom* (1924), contains a rather subjective account of his guerrilla years.

Ned Broy (1887–1972) was born in County Kildare and worked as a sergeant-clerk in the DMP from 1911. He became one of Collins's* most successful agents in the Castle, supplying him with early information about police intentions. He was arrested in February 1921 and jailed for six months. After the Treaty, he was made an adjutant in the air force and promoted to colonel. He succeeded Eoin O'Duffy (1892–1944) as commissioner of the Gardaí and formed an armed group of police to aid the confiscation of cattle from farmers who refused to pay rates; this group became known as 'Broy's Harriers'. He was always interested in athletics and became president of the Irish Olympic Council in 1935.

Cathal Brugha (1874–1922) was born Charles Burgess in Dublin and was severely wounded during Easter Week. He became Chief of Staff of the Volunteers in 1917, formally relinquishing the post to Richard Mulcahy when he became Minister of Defence in the first Dáil. It was due mainly to his efforts that the Volunteers and Sinn Féin became in practice indistinguishable. His motion of 20 August 1919 requiring all members to swear allegiance to the Irish republic established the IRA. He was the most vigorous opponent of the Treaty and, although crippled from earlier wounds, died as a result of a gun battle in Talbot Street in the second week of the Civil War.

Erskine Childers (1870–1922) was born in London but was reared in Wicklow. He was educated at Haileybury and Cambridge and saw service in the Boer War. An expert mariner (his novel *The Riddle of the Sands*, postulating a German invasion of Britain, was a best-seller in 1903 and has never been out of print since), he brought a shipment of arms for the Irish Volunteers into Howth in July 1914. He served in the Royal Navy air service during the Great War and succeeded Desmond Fitzgerald as director of publicity for the Volunteers during the War of Independence, editing the highly propagandist and extremely successful *Irish Bulletin*. Though a member of the Treaty delegation, he rejected the Treaty's terms and was executed by firing squad by government forces on 24 November 1922 for being in possession of a revolver, a gift from his friend Michael Collins*.

Sir Winston Churchill OM (1874–1965) was the eldest son of Lord Randolph Churchill and born in Blenheim Palace, the home of his grander relation, the Duke of Marlborough. While Minister of War and Air in Lloyd George's* coalition (1918–21), he advocated the criminalisation of IRA activities, refusing to regard them as a legitimate army at war, but he was an active member of the Treaty negotiations and strongly supported the Free State. After many years as a political maverick he became prime minister on the fall of Neville Chamberlain (1869–1940) and was one of the significant leaders in the Second World War. He refused all royal honours except the exclusive Order of Merit until his late acceptance of a knighthood and won the Nobel Prize for Literature in 1953.

Michael Collins (1890–1922) was born in Clona-kilty, County Cork, and served as a clerk in the British civil service in London. He joined the IRB in 1915 and was one of the survivors of Easter Week. By the time he was released from Frongoch in December 1916 he was already an important leader in the movement and he played an important part its reorganisation. During the War of Independence he was a brilliant if ruthless head of military intelligence. He was a reluctant member of the Treaty delegation but regarded the terms as the best that were possible in the circumstances. Though he had little experience of actual guerrilla fighting, he was the obvious choice for commander-in-chief of the Free State forces during the Civil War. He was killed in an ambush in Béal na mBláth, not far from his birthplace, on 22 August 1922.

Sir Alfred Cope (1880–1954), known popularly as 'Andy', was a career politician and served as assistant under-secretary to Sir Hamar Green-wood* during the War of Independence. He was one of the most active and successful parties in bringing about the Truce that finished the war and he assisted General Macready in supervising the withdrawal of British troops. He was knighted in 1922.

Frank Percy Crozier (1879–1937) was a dashing career soldier of Ulster extraction who fought in both the Boer War and the Great War, training the UVF in the interval. He rose to the rank of brigadier and was active in both the Lithuanian and Polish armies against the Bolsheviks. He assumed command of the Auxiliary cadets but resigned in February 1921 when his attempts to discipline the force were frustrated by General Tudor. He wrote a number of books of memoirs, including *Ireland for Ever* (1932), which was remarkably pro-nationalist.

Liam Deasy (1898–1974) was born near Bandon in County Cork and was adjutant of the West Cork Brigade. His account of the brigade's activities in *Towards Ireland Free* (1973) is somewhat at variance in detail with that of Tom Barry's. Remembered by Lt Col F. W. Crake, who was killed at Kilmichael, for his 'soldierly humanity', he took the anti-Treaty side in the

Civil War but had no relish for the struggle. Captured by Free State forces in 1923, he was happy to sign a call for unconditional surrender. After the war he took no further part in public life but served throughout the Emergency in the Irish army.

Éamon de Valera (1882–1974) was born in New York but was brought up in Ireland from the age of two. He became a mathematics lecturer and joined the Gaelic League in 1908 and the IRB in 1913. Commander of the garrison at Boland's Mills during Easter Week, he was the only 1916 leader to survive execution, largely due to the efforts of John Redmond and John Dillon. He was president of the first Dáil Éireann but spent much of the War of Independence in America, speaking on behalf of Ireland's right to full self-government and collecting large sums of money for the cause. The first Irish leader to meet Lloyd George* after the Truce, he would not be part of the Treaty delegation and rejected the terms of the agreement made by Griffith* and Collins*, suggesting an alternative that was refused by the British government. Though inactive during the Civil War, he signed the order of cessation in 1923. He created a political party, Fianna Fáil, out of the residual republicans, and led it as Taoiseach in four governments. He also served two terms as president (1959–73).

Éamonn Duggan (1874–1936) was born in County Meath and qualified as a solicitor in 1914. He was arrested after the Easter Rising and became director of IRA intelligence. He was elected to the first Dáil in 1918; he was imprisoned in 1920 but was subsequently released, to take part in the Mansion House talks that led to the Truce. He was one of the signatories of the Treaty and held several posts in Cosgrave's government, retiring in 1933 to become a senator.

John Denton French, First Earl of Ypres (1852–1925) was born in Kent into a family with property in County Roscommon. He joined the Royal Navy when he was fourteen but later transferred to the army. After a successful career as a cavalry officer in the Sudan and during the Boer War, he became Chief Inspector of the Garda Síochána in

1911. Forced to resign because of his support for the anti-Home Rule officers in the Curragh, he was recalled to lead the British Expeditionary Force in 1914, when the Great War began. General Douglas Haig (1861–1928) replaced him because of his lack of diplomatic skills and his inability to liaise with the French army. He was made Lord Lieutenant of Ireland in 1918, resigning in 1921 with a gratuity of £50,000 after a period of office in which he demonstrated his lack of understanding of the Irish situation. During this period many attempts were made on his life, the most dangerous one involving the Squad, with Dan Breen* and Sean Treacy*, on 19 December 1919.

Frank Gallagher (1893–1962) was born in Cork and was deputy to Erskine Childers* on the staff of the Volunteer propaganda news-sheet the *Irish Bulletin,* which presented the activities of the IRA in the best possible light and was extremely influential in winning international support for the Irish cause. He was the first editor of the *Irish Press* (1931–95) and later worked for Radio Éireann and the National Library.

Arthur Griffith (1871–1922) was born in Dublin and became a journalist, a member of the Gaelic League and the IRB. With Bulmer Hobson (1883–1969), he founded Sinn Féin, which advocated Irish self-sufficiency and passive resistance as the best means of ending British Rule. He opposed the Home Rule bill of 1914 and was arrested after the Easter Rising, although he had not been a participant in it. Released at the general amnesty, he was re-arrested at the time of the 'German Plot' in 1918. He was elected MP for East Cavan while still in prison and was acting president of the Dáil while de Valera* was in America (1919–20). He was arrested in November 1920 but was released shortly before the truce in July 1921. He led the Treaty delegation in December of that year and was its first signatory. Elected president of the Dáil when de Valera resigned, he died of a cerebral haemorrhage on 12 August 1921, worn out by the strain of the negotiations and the Civil War which greeted the rejection of the Treaty terms.

David Lloyd George (1863–1945) was born in Manchester but was brought up in Criccieth in Gwynedd. He had a brilliant career as a Liberal reformer, associated with old-age pensions, National Insurance and the taming of the House of Lords. He was Minister of Munitions, Secretary for War and, having ousted Asquith, prime minister from 1916, proving a highly efficient war leader. Usually in sympathy with the Ulster unionists, he decided on exclusion on their terms as early as 1916, and his dealings with the nationalist Irish were vitiated by the instinctive and deep suspicion of one Celtic race for another. Slow to give the War of Independence the political attention it deserved, he tried an ineffectual mixture of conciliation and coercion until forced to seek an end to the struggle through the truce. It was his threat of 'war within three days' that persuaded Griffith and Collins to accept the Treaty terms. The 'Irish Question' helped force his resignation as prime minister in 1922.

Sir Hamar Greenwood (1870–1948) was born in Canada and came to live in England in 1895. He was called to the bar in 1906 and was elected as a Liberal MP in the same year. He took silk in 1910 and served in France in the Great War (1914–16). He was appointed Chief Secretary to Ireland on 12 April 1920 and, though it caused him some private embarrassment, he publicly defended the excesses of the Tans and Auxiliaries. He took little part in the pre-truce talks, though he was present during the Treaty negotiations. Made a baronet in 1915, he followed Churchill to join the Conservative Party and became a viscount in 1937.

Sir Cecil Francis Nevil Macready (1862–1945) was born in Aberdeen, the son of the great Shakespearean actor William Macready (1793–1873), himself of Irish extraction, who sired him at age sixty-four. He joined the Gordon Highlanders and was GOC Belfast before becoming adjutant to Lord French* in the British Expeditionary Force. Promoted to brigadier rank in 1918, he served as Commissioner of the Metropolitan Police (1918–20) before being persuaded to accept the post of General Officer Commanding in Ireland by his old commander, Lord French*. Though disclaiming any trace of Irishness, his code of military conduct made him publicly decry the behaviour of the Black and Tans and the Auxies. He was active in seeking the basis for a truce, was present at discussions with de Valera*, Griffith* and Jan Christian Smuts* in July 1921 and worked out the terms of the Truce with Robert Barton* and Éamonn Duggan*. He oversaw the withdrawal of British forces in January 1922 and retired from the army in 1923.

Tomás Mac Curtain (1884–1920) was born in County Cork and was a member (and teacher) in the Gaelic League and, with Terence MacSwiney*, organised the Cork Volunteers in preparation for the Easter Rising. After his release from internment, he was active in the movement, becoming the first Sinn Féin lord mayor of Cork. He was assassinated by a gang of masked raiders – almost certainly Black and Tans. The coroner's verdict blamed, among others, Lloyd George* and DI Swanzy for his death.

Terence MacSwiney (1879–1920) was born in Cork and, with Tomás Mac Curtain organised the Volunteers in anticipation of the Easter Rising. He succeeded MacCurtain as lord mayor of Cork after the latter's death in March 1920.

Arrested under the Defence of the Realm Act on 19 August 1920, he went on hunger strike in Brixton. He died on 24 October after seventy-four days on hunger strike, during which all appeals for his release had gone unheeded, but the publicity surrounding his protracted death was very damaging to Britain's reputation in Europe, Australia and America. His funeral in London had a guard of honour of Volunteers in prohibited uniform and the streets were filled with mourners, not all of them Irish exiles.

Jan Christian Smuts (1870–1950) was born in Cape Colony and led the guerrilla forces in the Boer War (1899–1902). He was a key figure in the peace negotiations and in the setting up of the Union of South Africa in 1910. He served in the British war cabinets in both world wars but was unable to overcome the rise of Afrikaans nationalism. The defeat of his pro-Commonwealth United Party by the National Party in 1948 led, in 1967, to the setting up of the union as a republic outside the Commonwealth. He was one of the prime movers in arranging the truce that ended the war in 1921 and is credited as the main architect of the speech of George V at the opening of the Northern Ireland parliament on 22 June 1921 that helped persuade the British to make every effort to secure a cessation.

Sean Treacy (1895–1920) was a leading Gaelic League organiser in South Tipperary and a member of the Irish Volunteers. With Dan Breen* he led the Soloheadbeg ambush that began the War of Independence. He and Breen were involved in an attempt to assassinate the Viceroy, Lord French*, in Dublin in December 1919. He was killed in a gun battle in Talbot Street, Dublin, on 14 October 1920.

Hugh H. Tudor (1871–1965) was born in Exeter and was wounded in action in both the Boer and the Great Wars. Appointed chief of the Irish police services in 1920, holding his military rank of major general, he oversaw the enlargement of the RIC with Black and Tans and Auxiliary cadets. He was constant in his defence of the new recruits but admitted that there was much drunkenness and indiscipline among them, blaming it on the conditions under which they had to operate. He initiated the use of the aeroplane as a counter-terrorist weapon and was subsequently air vice-marshal and general officer commanding in Palestine, bringing with him many of his execrated personnel.

SELECT BIBLIOGRAPHY

Abbott, R. *Police Casualties in Ireland. 1919–1922*. Dublin & Cork, 2000.

Barry T. *Guerrilla Days in Ireland*. Cork, 1958.

Breen, D. *My Fight for Irish Freedom*, Dublin, 1924 (revised 1964).

Coogan, T. P. *Michael Collins*. London, 1990.

Deasy, L. *Towards Ireland Free*. Cork, 1973.

Doherty, G. and Keogh, D. (eds.) *Michael Collins and the Making of the Irish State*. Dublin, 1998.

Dwyer, T. Ryle. *De Valera: The Man and the Myths*. Dublin, 1991.

——————.*Michael Collins: 'The Man Who Won the War'*. Cork, 1990.

Griffith, K. and O'Grady, T. (eds.) *Curious Journey*. Cork, 1998.

Hart, P. *The IRA and Its Enemies*. Oxford, 1998.

Kee, R. *The Green Flag*. London, 1970.

Macardle, D. *The Irish Republic*. Dublin, 1937 (revised 1968).

Neligan, D. *The Spy in the Castle*. London, 1968.

O'Malley, E. *On Another Man's Wound*. Dublin, 1936.